# Roadmap to the Zone:

## Enhancing Athletic Performance

By

### Robert S. Neff, Ph.D. and
### Michael K. Garza, Ed.D.

authorHOUSE

*1663 Liberty Drive, Suite 200*
*Bloomington, Indiana 47403*
*(800) 839-8640*
*www.authorhouse.com*

First published by AuthorHouse 07/30/04


ISBN: 1-4184-7968-3 (sc)


Library of Congress Control Number: 2004095222

Printed in the United States of America
Bloomington, Indiana

This book is printed on acid-free paper.

For additional copies of this book or for private sport psychology training, contact:

Robertneff.com
2111 Rheims Dr.
Carrollton, Texas 75006
Fax: 972-416-0712
email@robertneff.com

Copyeditor: Eric Tate
Assistant Editors: Heidi Smith and Erik Neff
Cover Design: Janie Montague and Marie St. Hilaire

Our gratitude goes to our families and loved ones for their continued encouragement and support. We are a couple of very fortunate guys!

Special thanks to Dion Crupi for his assistance during the developmental stages of the concepts presented in this book.

# About the Authors

Robert S Neff, Ph.D.  Dr. Neff is a former multi-sport college varsity athlete who later competed on the professional tennis tour. He earned his Ph.D. in sport psychology from the department of Kinesiology at Michigan State University and is the current President of the American Association of Applied Sport Psychology. As a college professor, Dr. Neff teaches sport psychology courses and consults privately in the Dallas area with athletes of all sports and ages. He has made it his career mission to simplify sport psychology concepts so athletes and coaches can more effectively use them in their training and competitions. He remains a certified USPTA Teaching Professional and USTA High Performance Coach.

Michael K. Garza, Ed.D.  Dr. Garza received his Counseling Psychology doctoral degree from Texas A&M in Commerce, Texas. For over 25 years, Dr. Garza operated a private consulting and psychotherapy practice. He is currently a full-time psychology professor in the Dallas County Community College District. As a competitive tennis player, Dr. Garza has been ranked nationally for over 20 years, playing both singles and doubles. He is a past president of the Dallas Tennis Association, past president of the Dallas Business Association, past president of Fathers for Equal Rights, and has just recently started a regional chapter for Children and Adults with Attention Deficit Disorder in the Dallas area.

# Upcoming Books from these Authors

*Setting Life Goals*: How to achieve what you really want in life

*Roadmap to the Tennis Zone*: Tennis specific directions to find the zone

*Roadmap to the Golf Zone*: Golf specific directions to find the zone

*Roadmap to the Sales Zone*: Information to help sales people excel

*Sport Psychology for Kids*: Short stories kids will remember and use

*Cognition and Nutrition for High Performance*: How food and thought affect emotions

**Visit us on the web at:** http://www.roadmaptothezone.com

Read this book carefully and you'll find a username and password to a protected page designed exclusively for book-owners.

This book is dedicated to all you athletes out there who

know you've got what it takes... and are ready to prove it.

x

# Forward

Although the expression "sports-junkie" had not been coined when I was a kid, I was one. Whatever was available that involved running, throwing, hitting, kicking, etc., I was there. I even did the play-by-play announcing simultaneously with my play, mimicking radio announcers of that era.

One of many differences between then and now is that none of the sports playing I did then was organized. Everything was pick-up, or, as happened many days when there was no opportunity for a pick-up game, I played solo. I used a wall or an empty field – not a well-groomed field with a fence - just a scratchy piece of ground that might have had things sitting on it or even growing on it like trees.

All of this is not recited to evoke sympathy, but to establish a base period for comparison purposes in terms of the level of comprehensiveness and sophistication that has been reached in sports today versus what existed decades ago. It is astounding to recall the bygone days of just-roll-out-of-the-house-and-play. In addition to not having a high quality venue (field, gym or court), there were no uniforms or protective equipment. Whatever was available was used, typically just a ball (and tattered as opposed to new).

Fast forward to today's world of sports. Technology has brought us incredible equipment. We have complete access to quality coaching and coaching techniques. We are given clear direction about nutrition and proper diet to maximize performance. And, training of all types is in vogue (physical fitness, strength training, agility, core, massage, cross training). In light of all this, doesn't it seem natural that one would ask the question, "Has everything possible been covered to foster maximum sports performance by individuals?"

The answer would be, "Not quite." What about the mind? More specifically, what about training of the mind in order to take maximum advantage of all the other enhancements that have contributed to athletic performance preparation and implementation?" Voila! Along come Drs. Neff and Garza with their "Roadmap to the Zone."

In the latter stages of my life, I have gravitated from a 'player-of-all-sports' to tennis as my participation sport, even while maintaining my status as a sports-junkie. Along the way, I have experienced the truism that in all sports, at all ages, there are multiple levels of competition. Obviously, competition encompasses both the enjoyment that comes from the play AND the pursuit of excellence. The higher the level of competition, the more one finds parity of skill levels amongst individual and team competitors. This leads inevitably to a quest for an "edge" to facilitate winning.

In tennis, frequently that edge can come from mental preparation and/or mental tenacity employed throughout the course of a match. Having experienced that, and still being a fierce competitor, even at an advanced age, I jumped at the opportunity to read an early draft of this book and was flattered by the invitation to write this Forward. We all aspire to perform in "The Zone." Having this "Roadmap" to get us to that magical place should be welcomed and will prove to be invaluable, in my opinion. There are many worthwhile explanations and tips provided herein to assist us in getting to our desired performance level.

In summary, I urge you to absorb the whole "Roadmap to The Zone." Whether you will use some or all of it in your athletic pursuits is up to you. My one deep-thought inquiry to you as an athlete is, "If you really want to win, can you afford to yield the mental skills ground, a potential "edge," to your opponent?!" If not, read on...

**D. Lee Hamilton, Executive Director & Chief Operating Officer United States Tennis Association**

# Table of Contents

"The credit belongs to the man who is actually in the arena, whose face is marred by dust and sweat and blood; who strives valiantly; who errs and comes short again and again, who knows the great enthusiasms, the great devotions, and spends himself in a worthy cause; who at best, knows the triumph of high achievement; and who, at the worst, if he fails, at least fails while daring greatly, so that his place shall never be with those cold and timid souls who know neither victory nor defeat."

-Theodore Roosevelt, "Citizen in a Republic", April 23, 1910

# Introduction

Sport psychology has come a long way in the past decade. Motivated by the stories of athletes overcoming impossible odds to succeed (see the 'Inspirational Stories' section for a few of them), many researchers and coaches have dedicated their careers to finding out how to best prepare for, and what to think about during, competition. This book was written for athletes and any other performer who is searching for detailed "directions" on their journey toward understanding high performance and attaining their biggest dreams.

Using the analogy of a "Roadmap," we have assumed that everyone reading this book is embarking on a journey to the same destination. That destination is the "Performance Zone," or simply, THE ZONE. The Zone has for years been described as a highly illusive state of being where performance happens automatically, effortlessly, favorably, but also randomly. Controlling the Zone is compared to controlling the weather - things seem to happen by chance, even illogically. Why is it that we tend to find the Zone when we don't care as much about finding it? Why does the Zone go away as soon as we acknowledge that it's there? If you have found the Zone, you likely know it to be a highly pleasurable place filled with confidence, focus and enjoyment. You probably recall very few distractions, no fear of making errors, and no thought of the potential outcome. If you've found the Zone once, you want it every time you compete.

On this journey to the Zone, we travelers need to know which path to follow, what to experience along the way, when to turn, and what to expect next. Similarly, we have attempted to give clear directions about which psychological skills to use, their benefits, and how to practice them so you can improve the chances of Zoning.

While we may all be going to the same destination, we acknowledge that different people will choose different paths. This is a necessary reality on the road to enhancing one's performance. Everyone has different strengths and weaknesses as well as varying motives to succeed. The skills discussed in this book will be combined by each individual in various ways that make the most sense for that individual. We endeavor to give guidelines along the way, much like a travel agent. As any successful travel agent does, we use our years of experience to provide an 'ideal' roadmap to follow so that your goals are met in the most beneficial way.

Here's an obvious statement, but a hugely important one: Before you can embark on any journey, you need to know where you're going. We find that most athletes have left the station and they're not sure which train they're on! So, it makes sense that goal setting should be our first chapter. We've developed an easy and straight-forward way to set, follow and update what you're trying to accomplish.

After you know where you're going, it will help if you can imagine yourself making the journey successfully. In this imagination process, you will not only more fully believe that you can succeed at the journey, you will be better prepared for the potential difficulties that all journeys entail. As such, Chapter 2 will discuss visualization.

Next, as you experience these difficulties (adversity), you will need to be strong enough to get yourself through it. What you tell yourself in the face of this adversity will be a big factor in how hard and how long you will persist. Chapter 3 will cover ideal self-talk.

Adversity is not only likely to occur, but necessary for you to become strong enough to perform at the highest levels of your sport or activity. Much of this 'strength' comes in the form of emotional strength. It is critical all performers understand how their emotions can be controlled by their thoughts. Chapter 4 puts it all together so you can quickly remind yourself of the critical components necessary for finding the zone. A new "flow diagram" of emotion control is presented here for the first time. It describes a path you can take to find the zone once your competition has started.

Finally, Chapter 5 serves as a 'follow-through' chapter, helping you build these skills and concepts into your weekly training regimen. After you complete this book, you'll have a custom-designed mental skills training program that can be changed and updated as you reach each of your goals.

Let's get started!

# Chapter 1:
# Where Are You Going?

*"If one does not know to which port he is sailing, no wind is favorable."* Seneca

## Creating the Roadmap

Before beginning any journey, it's critical you know where you want to go, why you want to go there, what roadblocks will likely get in your way, and how you will try to solve those problems if you encounter them. Let's imagine you want to drive to Canada for a vacation. If you've made the trip before, or have someone with you who has, it's a huge advantage. If not, a company like AAA can create a detailed map showing exactly where to go and even when to detour to avoid construction and traffic. You can easily look ahead and make plans to avoid problem areas.

After you finish the worksheets in this chapter, you will have constructed a roadmap to your highest dreams. You will know where you are going and what you will have to do along the way. This will be your first draft that will get more detailed with experience and by applying what you learn from others who have gone before you. Read biographies of greats in your sport. Find experienced coaches who have gone to where you are headed or have helped others to get there. As you gain this knowledge of what difficulties to expect during your journey, you'll be able to create solutions long before problems ever happen. Even if you can't avoid a problem, you'll have a plan to get you through it. The following chapters will provide solutions to common mental roadblocks encountered by athletes with high goals.

"The difference between the successful person and the unsuccessful person is the unsuccessful person stops short of his goals, the successful person surpasses his goals."
Joseph Martino

One of the most important factors that drive people to be successful is their "WHY." Why are they doing what they're doing? Why did Michael Jordan, for example, work so hard at his basketball skills even after people acknowledged him as one of the best players in the game? Why was he always the first to practice and the last to leave? Why did he continue doing his weights on game days and even during the playoffs? Was it because he was trying to prove something to his high school coach who cut him from the team? Was it because he wanted an NBA championship ring? Three rings in a row? Was it because he wanted to be known as the best player of all-time? Whatever it is, Jordan and every other great athlete have strong reasons WHY they compete.

## The Bigger the Why

When you have a big enough 'Why' the 'How' becomes easy. Talk show host Oprah Winfrey once interviewed a man who had a big 'Why.' His daughter was dying and needed a kidney transplant. He wanted to donate one of his, but he was obese and the doctors refused. They said he had to lose 100 pounds in 8 months. He had been trying for years to lose weight but couldn't do it. He was in good company - there are millions of people who can't seem to lose any weight. But this man did it - and with a month to spare. He said it was easy because he had such an important reason why - to save his daughter. As soon as his 'why' was big enough, the 'how' became clear, and even easy.

**'Why' Examples from Successful Athletes:** Prove it to myself or others; Like achieving; Like improving; Want praise, admiration or approval; To be attractive to others; Take care of others; Give thanks; Show respect to God for giving skills; Leave a legacy; Make the world a better place; To be happy; To feel good about self; Have more time; Have more money;

Become healthier; Improve a life; Save a life. Why will you go through all the sacrifice and pain to be successful?

**A) List your 5 biggest sport-related dreams and why each is important to you.**

| DREAMS | WHY |
|---|---|
| 1) | 1) |
| 2) | 2) |
| 3) | 3) |
| 4) | 4) |
| 5) | 5) |

Additional goal sheets can be found at: http://www.roadmaptothezone.com

## B) For each dream, list the biggest potential roadblocks you may face, and then the best solutions.

| ROADBLOCKS | SOLUTIONS |
|---|---|
| Dream 1)<br>a)<br>b)<br>c)<br>d)<br>e) | a)<br>b)<br>c)<br>d)<br>e) |
| Dream 2)<br>a)<br>b)<br>c)<br>d)<br>e) | a)<br>b)<br>c)<br>d)<br>e) |
| Dream 3)<br>a)<br>b)<br>c)<br>d)<br>e) | a)<br>b)<br>c)<br>d)<br>e) |
| Dream 4)<br>a)<br>b)<br>c)<br>d)<br>e) | a)<br>b)<br>c)<br>d)<br>e) |
| Dream 5)<br>a)<br>b)<br>c)<br>d)<br>e) | a)<br>b)<br>c)<br>d)<br>e) |

Additional goal sheets can be found at: http://www.roadmaptothezone.com

# C) Create your <u>ROADMAP</u> to your highest dream.

Here's an example of what you're about to create using the goals you've just written in A) and B):

**"Roadmap" Goalsheet**

Name: _____     Today's Date: _12 / 7 / 2003_

| | Dreams and Goals | | Target Date |
|---|---|---|---|
| 19 y.o | Quality for USA Olympic Team | | Sept 2012 |
| 18 y.o. | Top 3 at World Championships | | June 2011 |
| 16 y.o | Quality for National Team | Top 4 at VISA Cup | June 2004 |
| 15 y.o. | Quality for VISA Cup | Olympic Alternate | June 2008 |
| 13 y.o | Quality for Elite Level | | May 2007 |
| 12 y.o | Top 3 at Level 10 State | | October 2006 |
| 11 y.o. | Quality for Level 10 | | June 2005 |
| 11 y.o | Place Top 3 at Level 9 State | | April 2005 |
| 10 y.o | Quality for Level 9 | | April 2004 ✓ |

Update by: _2 / 7 / 04_ (every 60 days)

## Directions for Creating Your Roadmap:

1) The form on the next page is what you should now draw on a blank piece of paper (or, you can download it from http://www.roadmaptothezone.com.
2) Write your biggest sport-related dream (from A earlier). We're asking you to 'start with the end in mind,' so make sure this dream is the final major accomplishment you hope to achieve.
3) Put a box around it at the top of the page.
4) Draw a short arrow pointing up at the bottom of this box.
5) Work down the page writing the most significant accomplishment you will need to achieve in order to reach the higher box.
6) Continue until you get to present day (this lowest goal should be your next major accomplishment).
7) Now go back up the page writing in target dates in the right column for each goal.
8) Write in today's date, and the date 60 days from now when you will update this goal sheet.
9) Compare your 'Roadmap' goal sheet to the sample on the previous page. They should look similar.
10) Post this 'Roadmap' in a visible place (bathroom mirror, on the wall, in your locker, etc.). You want to see this sheet every day!

| Roadmap Goal Sheet | Target Date |
|---|---|
| | |

Update by: ___/___/___ (every 60 days)     Today's Date: ___/___/__

**"A goal is a dream with a deadline." Napoleon Hill**

### Do This Exercise (You'll use this later in Chapter 5)

Using the Roadmap you just created, make a short list of 5 key things you have to do to reach the <u>next goal</u> on your sheet. This list should include CONTROLLABLE things only. This is your action list. For example, if an athlete's next major goal is to qualify for the nationals, the action list might include things like improving fitness, improving a technical weakness, studying performance videos, reducing negative self-talk, scheduling tougher practice opponents, etc. Be specific about what you will do each week and by when.

Next Major Goal: _____

5 Key Things to Move Me to This Goal:

1)

2)

3)

4)

5)

"The most important thing you can do to achieve your goals is to make sure that as soon as you set them, you immediately begin to create momentum. The most important rules that I ever adopted to help me in achieving my goals were those I learned from a very successful man who taught me to first write down the goal, and then to never leave the site of setting a goal without first taking some form of positive action toward its attainment."
*- Anthony Robbins*

# Chapter 2:
# Visualization

*"Visualization was the key to my success."* Jack
Nicklaus, winner of 6 Masters and a record 18 Majors.
Sports Illustrated's 'Greatest Golfer of the Century'

## See It Before You Believe It

You know the old saying, "I'll believe it when I see it"? If you've ever said that to yourself, you probably meant that you didn't believe something was ever going to happen and that you'd need to see it first. Unfortunately, high performance doesn't quite work that way. In fact, anybody who ever achieved anything of significance "saw" it in their mind first (imagined it) and then believed it was possible to bring into reality. Examples include: Bannister breaking the 4-minute mile; Armstrong landing on the moon; Bell inventing the telephone; and the Wright Brothers succeeding at manned flight. In every case, these people clearly saw in their minds that it was possible before anyone else believed it. They had a mental picture of what they were going to do long before they actually did it. Imagining it enhanced their belief that it was possible to do. This process of creating an ideal image in your mind to improve the chances of it actually happening is called visualization.

---

**Visualization is Key**, by Neil Eskelin

Do you believe our imagination has much to do with success? Arnold Schwarzenegger won the title of Mr. Universe seven times. But he didn't keep his title by only pumping iron. As part of his workout routine, he would frequently go into the corner of the gym and visualize himself winning the title again. Jack Nicklaus, the great professional golfer, explained his imaging technique. He said, "First I 'see' the ball where I want it to finish - nice and white and sitting up high on the bright green grass. Then the scene quickly changes, and I 'see' the ball going there; its path, trajectory and shape, even its behavior on the landing. Then," says Nicklaus, "there's sort of a fade-out, and the next scene shows me making the kind of swing that will turn the previous images into reality."

---

13

## What is Visualization (or visual imagery)?

It's a picture in our mind; the picture being like a movie and our mind like a screen. You have control over what you want to put on the screen. It is something that should be done along with physical practicing (you can't perform consistently well without actually going out and physically practicing), but you also need to visualize clearly in order to perform well. Visual imagery practiced consistently will help you to perform the physical skills better.

## Why Would I Practice Visualizing?

The first reason is to learn skills or sequences that occur in competition (visualizing strengthens the neural pathways - nerves fire almost exactly the same as if you were really physically doing the activity). Next, you might visualize to practice skills or sequences you've recently learned. Visualization also can be used to control nervousness (the more times you see the ideal happening, the more confident you will feel - also, practicing remaining calm makes it more likely you'll make that choice when you feel stress). Finally, athletes often use visualization to help remember skills or sequences during periods of injury (visualizing makes it easier to perform after healing).

## 18 Holes in Mind

Major James Nesmeth had a dream of improving his golf game, and he developed a unique method of achieving his goal. Until he devised this method, he was just your average weekend golfer, shooting in the mid to low nineties. Then, for seven years, he completely quit the game. He never touched a club. He never set foot on a fairway.

Ironically, it was during this seven-year break from the game that Major Nesmeth came up with his amazingly effective technique for improving his game - a technique we can all learn from. In fact, the first time he set foot on a golf course after his hiatus from the game, he shot an astonishing 74! He had cut 20 strokes off his average without having swung a golf club in seven years! Unbelievable. Not only that, but his physical condition had actually deteriorated during those seven years. What was Major Nesmeth's secret? Visualization. You see, Major Nesmeth had spent those seven years as a prisoner of war in North Vietnam. During those seven years, he was imprisoned in a cage that was approximately four and one-half feet high and five feet long.

During almost the entire time he was imprisoned, he saw no one, talked to no one and experienced no physical activity. During the first few months he did virtually nothing but hope and pray for his release. Then he realized he had to find some way to occupy his mind or he would lose his sanity and probably his life. That's when he learned to visualize. In his mind, he selected his hometown golf course and started playing golf. Every day, he played a full 18 holes in his mind. He experienced everything to the last detail. He saw himself dressed in his golf clothes. He smelled the fragrance of the trees and the freshly trimmed grass. He experienced different weather conditions - windy spring days, overcast winter days, and sunny summer mornings. In his imagination, every detail of the tee, the individual blades of grass, the trees, the singing birds, the scampering squirrels, and the lay of the course became totally clear.

He felt the grip of the club in his hands. He instructed himself as he practiced smoothing out his down-swing and the follow-through on his shot. Then he watched the ball arc down the exact center of the fairway, bounce a couple of times and roll to the exact spot he had selected, all in his mind. In the real world, he was in no hurry. He had no place to go. So in his mind, he took every step on his way to the ball, just as if he were physically on the course. It took him just as long in imaginary time to play 18 holes as it would have taken in reality. Not a detail was omitted. Not once did he ever miss a shot. He never hooked or sliced. He never missed putt. He did what most people wished they could do - he played eighteen holes of gold seven days a week, four hours a day. Seven years. Twenty strokes off. True story.

## How Do I Visualize?

Visualization is much clearer and more controllable when people are calm (no tightness, anger or nervousness). To help you learn to control your muscle tension, it's good to practice a relaxation sequence that teaches your body to re-lax whenever you need (see Appendix A and B). Some people struggle with visualizing, but everyone can do it quite well. Try visualizing as you read the sentence below. Be sure to visualize looking out of your own eyes (1st person) instead of as an observer watching yourself. First person visualizing allows the images to be very similar to what you'd actually see if you were doing it, and, it enables you to actually FEEL what it's like (kinesthetic response). Read this sentence and visualize actually doing what it describes:

*"You are in your bedroom where you live. You are sitting on your bed. Stand up and walk over to the door. Reach out and open the door. Notice which hand you used. See the type of handle on the door and imagine feeling the breeze creat-ed by the door passing in front of your face. Go through the door and walk to the kitchen. See what is on the walls as you go. Imagine you are bare foot and feel the floor surface(s) as you walk. Turn on the kitchen light and walk over to the fridge. Open the door and see that the fridge is empty ex-cept for a jar of dill pickles. You are hungry and thirsty. Take the jar out and feel how heavy and cold the jar is. Twist off the top and hear the 'pop' sound. Take a pickle out. It's cold*

*and slimy. Take a big bite. Hear the crunch sound and taste the pickle. Now pick up the jar with both hands and take a big drink of the cold pickle juice."*

Most people have never done what this sentence describes! However, you probably imagined doing it just fine! The point is, even if you've never performed well in front of a large audience, for example, you CAN imagine doing so. Visualizing being successful will then make it easier for you to actually perform successfully in front of large audiences!

**Visualization Practice Ideas**

Use the descriptions below to improve the quality of your mental images. It should be easiest to imagine familiar objects and short trips you take often. Visualizing far away or imaginary locations can be more challenging if you've never been to them. Many people imagine beautiful locations while they try to calm themselves down. Lastly, visualize performing your sport or activity. Because of the changing nature of sport, it is easier to tape record sequences that are most likely to happen and then visualize them being done successfully. However, many athletes imagine themselves performing well in front of large crowds and dealing with all the adversity that would actually occur. This helps them to feel more comfortable when they are actually in that competitive situation.

**1) Objects:** Visualize these to increase your control over images. <u>Directions</u>: look at the object, then close your eyes and try to see the shape and color clearly:

    a) your shoes;
    b) a ball;
    c) tooth paste container;
    d) a car;
    e) any other object that seems interesting;

**2) Trips:** Visualize to improve your ability to see details. <u>Directions</u>: Imagine yourself going somewhere and pay attention to what is there (things, colors and smells)

> a) walk from your bedroom to your kitchen;
> b) drive from home to work or school;
> c) take a walk around the outside of your house;
> d) run one lap around the track (actually time yourself);
> e) imagine anything involving you moving somewhere;

**3) Locations:** These are usually used to relax or motivate. <u>Directions</u>: Imagine yourself being somewhere and then try to actually make your body experience it (scenery, temperature, sounds, and smells)

> a) lying on a warm sandy beach with a cool ocean breeze
> b) sitting in the middle of an open field full of flowers
> c) sitting in an outside hot tub with snow falling all around you
> d) hiking through a valley surrounded by enormous mountains
> e) any place that might relax you

**4) Performance:** The following are examples of how to practice visualizing performances. Athletes routinely do this to increase success during competition. <u>Directions</u>: Imagine a situation that you want to improve and then make it go well for you (if it starts to go bad, say STOP!, rewind the tape and play it until you see yourself do it properly). Here are some examples of how to do performance visualization:

a) Tennis: Imagine you are the server. Hit the serve out wide, the return comes back cross-court short, you approach with topspin down the line, the pass goes cross-court, and you volley down the line to win the point.

b) Golf: Imagine you are on the 18th hole, Par 5. Be sure to visualize the exact pre-shot and post-shot routine that you use when actually on the course. With your driver, you hit the ball straight down the fairway 300 yards. Your second shot is a 2 iron that you hit to within 20 yards of the green. Your third shot is a wedge that you chip within 6 feet of the hole. You put in for a birdie.

c) Basketball: Imagine you are in a close game with only seconds to play. The ball comes to you and you shoot an 18-foot jumper that goes in. You were fouled on the play and the score is now tied with no time left. You go to the foul line confidently, go through your pre-shot routine, visualize a perfect shot and then make it to win the game.

*"I study pitchers. I visualize pitches. That gives me a better chance every time I step into the box. That doesn't mean I'm going to get a hit every game, but that's one of the reasons I've come a long way as a hitter." - **Mark McGwire (Hit 70 home runs to beat Roger Maris' record of 61)***

**Do This Exercise** (You'll use this later in Chapter 5)

A) Write down the 5 most common sequences or actions that occur in your sport (Examples: Tennis – serve & volley, return & pass, approach & volley, volley & overhead, forehand cross then backhand cross; Basketball – pick & roll, give & go, block out & rebound, dribble & shoot, pass & cut).

1)

2)

3)

4)

5)

B) Write down the 3 sequences or actions you need to improve most or that you need to execute well to win. We will use these 3 in the last chapter when we create a mental skills program for you.

1)

2)

3)

# Chapter 3:
# Self-Talk

*"The greatest mistake you can make in life is to be continually thinking you will make one."* Proverb

*"If you think you can, or if you think you cannot, you are right."* Henry Ford

One of the most frustrating things performers must deal with is negative self-talk. Imagine you are at an important competition. You have only a few minutes before you're on. Then it occurs to you, "What if I mess up! What if I perform badly and lose? What if..." Suddenly you get so nervous you have trouble breathing. These kinds of self-doubts contribute to stage fright, choking and under-performance. The good news is, we can learn to change and even block harmful self-talk that leads to nervousness and fear.

## You Are What You Say You Are

Everyone thinks negative thoughts at times. Only when people learn to _recognize_ negative thoughts, stop them, and replace them with positives will they be able to perform consistently well. If you tell yourself enough times that you are no good, you'll start believing it! Self-fulfilling prophecies are commonplace. Similarly, if you tell yourself you are a talented athlete, you will eventually believe this as well. The problem is, most athletes are not even aware of the thoughts they think during competition.

## The Mountain Story

A young boy and his father were walking in the mountains. The boy tripped and fell down a small hill and hurt himself. He yelled loudly in pain, "AAAAhhhhh!" He was surprised to hear a voice respond, "AAAAhhhhh!" Curiously he yelled, "Who are you?" and heard the answer, "Who are you?" He yelled again, "Shut-up you loser!" and heard the response back, "Shut-up you loser!" He got angry and screamed, "You're a coward!" but again heard back, "You're a coward." He didn't like being called a coward. By that time his father arrived, "Are you ok?" "Yes," the boy answered, "but I don't understand who's saying these mean things to me." His father smiled and said, "My son, pay attention." He then screamed, "You are awesome!" and voice responded, "You are awesome!" The boy is confused. The father explains, "What you hear is an echo, but it's really LIFE. It gives you back everything you say or do. Our life is simply a reflection of our actions. If you want more love in the world, decide to love more people. If you want more attention, give more attention to others." Life is not a coincidence. You get what you give.

## Thought Control Sequence

Use the following sequence to stop negative or self-destructive thoughts:

| RECOGNIZE the negative thought | Say "STOP" or "MAYBE" or "WHATEVER" | REPLACE with a positive word | Think STRATEGY |
|---|---|---|---|

The following 3 tables list common thoughts athletes have during competition. Use the first list to help you recognize the negative thoughts you have, and then the next two lists as ideas to replace the negative thoughts.

**Negatives After a Mistake:** The following is a list of negatives said after mistakes. This list is provided because most athletes don't realize they have negative self-talk. Before anything can be done to improve self-talk, you must first RECOGNIZE the negative. Feel free to add thoughts you have!

| I suck! | Ahhhhhhhh! | No Way! | Choker! |
|---|---|---|---|
| Any 4 letter word | Loser! | That was weak | Come ooooon! |
| I quit | I'm so bad | I'm the worst | You idiot! |
| I stink! | You're no athlete | I'm pitiful | How could I miss? |
| Why me? | Any sarcasm | What was that? | Just don't miss! |
| That was so easy! | I hate this sport! | Merry Christmas! | Oh, that's just great! |
|  |  |  |  |

**Positives After a Mistake:** This list of positives after mistakes is the most important list. Athletes can't always prevent errors from happening. All they can do is manage the mistake well, put it behind them, and move on with an optimistic outlook.

| Next point | Take your time | Keep fighting |
|---|---|---|
| Forget it | Calm down | High percentage |
| One at a time | Stay tough | Good effort |
|  |  |  |

**Other Helpful Words:** This list is just a series of shorter 'cue-words' you might use to replace the negative thought.

| Relax | React | Present |
|---|---|---|
| Focus | Quick | Fight |
| Control | Positive | Breathe |
|  |  |  |

**Thought Control Exercises**

1. **"Gap" Thinking:** This is a simple exercise to begin, but not easy to maintain. Close your eyes and become aware of your thoughts. Now become aware of the gaps between your thoughts. Try to stay in the gap between thoughts. When a thought comes in, simply recognize its existence and then get back into the gap. The length of time you stay in the gap is not as important as staying 'present' to the thoughts that come into your mind and 'refocusing' back into the gap.

2. **Past-Present-Future Labeling:** Write down thoughts you remember having before, during or after a competition. Now label them as past, present or future (Example of a past thought: "I can't believe I just made that mistake!"). Notice how negative emotions (anger, nervousness) are tied to thoughts that exist in the past or future. Positive emotions

(love, happiness, confidence...) are often present thoughts. Choose present thoughts during competition.

**3. Rational-Irrational Labeling**: Write down thoughts you remember having before, during or after a competition. Label them as rational (make sense) or irrational (make no sense). For example: "I always make that mistake!" That would be irrational because you don't ALWAYS make that mistake. Work at rewording your thoughts so they are rational and accurate ("I make that mistake when I get rushed. Be patient.").

**4. Perception-Reality Labeling**: This exercise involves you observing events in your world and describing them. Your goal is to describe only "What Happened" and not "Your Perception" of the event. For example: When describing a touchdown, it would be your perception if you said, "The QB threw the pass too hard and I was lucky to hang on to it." What happened was, "The QB threw a pass and I caught it for a touchdown." Notice how stating just the facts can reduce emotion surrounding an event.

**5. Other Labeling**: Helpful-Harmful (just recognizing how helpful or harmful a thought is can help); Permanent-Temporary (great athletes describe problems as temporary and successes as permanent); Lucky-Skillful (attributing success to luck is usually only done so one appears humble - great athletes consistently relate success to skill since it is more of a permanent factor); Controllable-Uncontrollable (successful athletes focus on factors they control - to do otherwise leads to feelings of helplessness and stress).

## A Description of Ideal Thoughts

**1. Before Competition**: Thoughts should be in the Present or slight future focusing on the ideal strategy. You should be sure to remain Rational, keeping thoughts simple and unemotional. Stay in <u>Reality</u>, on things you know to be true. All thoughts should be <u>Helpful</u> and supportive. If you can't <u>Control</u> it, don't worry about it.

**2. During Competition:** Work at staying in the <u>Gap</u> as much as possible. It is safe there since there are no thoughts to distract you or cause unwanted emotion. Perform on automatic as much as possible. If you have thoughts, keep them in the <u>Present</u>, <u>Helpful</u> and related to effort and strategy, which are both <u>Controllable</u> by you.

**3. After Competition:** To learn from what went on, you obviously need to get into the <u>Past</u> and evaluate your performance. Be constructive when criticizing and make sure a list of <u>Controllable</u> suggestions is made so you can take action on them immediately.

<u>**Become What You Want to Be**</u>, by Brian Cavanaugh

Let me tell you about a little girl who was born into a very poor family in a shack in the Backwoods of Tennessee. She was the 20th of 22 children, prematurely born and frail. Her survival was doubtful. When she was four years old she had double pneumonia and scarlet fever - a deadly combination that left her with a paralyzed and useless left leg. She had to wear an iron leg brace. Yet she was fortunate in having a mother who encouraged her. Well, this mother told her little girl, who was very bright, that despite the brace and leg, she could do whatever she wanted to do with her life. She told her that all she needed to do was to have faith, persistence, courage and indomitable spirit.

So at nine years of age, the little girl removed the leg brace, and she took the step the doctors told her she would never take normally. In four years, she developed a rhythmic stride, which was a medical wonder. Then this girl had the thought, the incredible thought, that she would like to be the world's greatest woman runner. At age 13, she entered a race. She came in last - way, way last. She entered every race in high school, and in every race she came in last. Everyone begged her quit! She didn't listen to the naysayers. She didn't accept the negative labels these people pinned on her. Everyday she reminded herself of her dream and what she had to do to get there. Then, one day, she came in next to last. And then there came a day when she won a race. From that day on, Wilma Rudolph won every race she entered.

Wilma went to Tennessee State University, where she met a coach named Ed Temple. Coach Temple saw her spirit, that she was a believer, and that she had great natural talent. He trained her hard and she went to the Olympic Games. There, she was pitted against the greatest woman runner of the day, a German girl named Jutta Heine. Nobody had ever beaten Jutta. But in the 100-meter dash, Wilma Rudolph won. She beat Jutta again in the 200-meters. Now Wilma had two Olympic gold medals. Finally came the 400-meter relay. It would be Wilma against Jutta once again. The first two runners on Wilma's team made perfect handoffs with the baton. But when the third runner handed the baton to Wilma, she was so excited she dropped it, and Wilma saw Jutta taking off down the track. It was impossible that anybody could catch this fleet and nimble girl. But Wilma did just that! Wilma Rudolph had earned three Olympic gold medals.

**Do This Exercise** (You'll use it later in Chapter 5)

Write down thoughts you remember having before, during or after a recent competition. Write as many as you can remember and write each thought on a separate line. Now label each thought as, 1) Past, Present or Future; 2) Rational or Irrational; 3) Perception or Reality; 4) Helpful or Harmful; and, 5) Temporary or Permanent.

Here's an example: "If I get a lead, I'll choke it away." Future; Irrational; Perception; Harmful, Permanent

## Recent Thoughts During Competition

| Thought | Past<br>Present<br>Future | Rational<br>Irrational | Perception<br>Reality | Helpful<br>Harmful | Temporary<br>Permanent |
|---|---|---|---|---|---|
|  |  |  |  |  |  |
|  |  |  |  |  |  |
|  |  |  |  |  |  |
|  |  |  |  |  |  |
|  |  |  |  |  |  |

Get more charts from: http://www.roadmaptothezone.com

# Chapter 4:
# Emotions and Zoning

*"The degree of one's emotions varies inversely with one's ability to think clearly." - Bertrand Russell*

*"THE ZONE does not <u>only</u> come to athletes randomly. Athletes enter the zone because of very specific reasons, and those reasons can be controlled." - Robert Neff*

**Putting It All Together**

So, to summarize what's been covered in this book so far, you know where you want to go; you know how you'll get there; you have a plan for overcoming adversity; you can imagine yourself succeeding; and, your self-talk is helping you. This chapter is about how to actually find the zone once your competition starts.

When athletes of all sports are "in the zone," they report feeling unbelievably confident about their ability to perform well. Even after mistakes, athletes feel as though they can bounce back with a high level of performance. Many report feeling excited, like children before opening presents. They can hardly wait to compete - to see what terrific combination of things they'll put together next. Athletes who are zoning often find themselves smiling regardless of how well they are doing because they are enjoying themselves so much. Pro golfer, Phil Mickelson demonstrated this perfectly as he smiled his way to a 2004 Masters win.

When describing how they feel, athletes often use words like: carefree, effortless, automatic, powerful, energized and simple. The following is a newspaper quote from a tennis player who had just won a tournament in California:

*"I wish I could control what just happened. I had confidence that I've never felt before - I really believed I could do ANYTHING! This is what it's all about - this is why I play tennis - not just to win tournaments - but to feel the way I did out there today. If I could feel that way more often, I'd be the best in the world."* This came from Pete Sampras, before he turned pro. Sampras went on to win more Grand Slams than any other man. Perhaps he learned how to control that 'feeling' that leads to the zone!

## How to Increase the Chances of Zoning

### Before the Competition

1) <u>Learn and Practice Efficient Technique</u>: Efficient movements have less tendency to break down during competition. Without technical efficiency, athletes rarely zone.

2) <u>Be in Terrific Physical Shape:</u> Zoning usually stops when athletes get tired (physically and/or mentally). Obviously fatigue, cramping and injury make zoning next to impossible. See Appendix H for more on dealing with sport-related injuries.

3) <u>Understand and Practice High Percentage Strategies</u>: No matter how great your technique and fitness levels are, athletes who consistently choose risky strategies cannot easily get themselves into the zone against athletes who know how to take advantage of tactical errors.

4) <u>Prepare Properly</u>: Make sure you've taken care of your equipment, diet, sleep, practice and pre-competition warm-up. Visualize daily using the information in the visualization chapter. See Appendix E for ideas on how to better use practice to prepare for competition.

### During the Competition

1) <u>Stay in the Present</u>: We don't know of any athlete in the history of sport who has zoned while they were angry or nervous. We don't believe it's even possible. By definition, a zoning athlete performs automatically, has high confidence, visualizes clearly and feels almost constant pleasure regardless of outcome. It is impossible to feel pleasure while dwelling on past mistakes or worrying about future outcomes.

Some players may continue to perform well while angry or nervous, but the highest level of performance, the zone, will not happen until negative emotion is eliminated.

2) <u>Keep Thoughts Positive and Helpful</u>: As soon as athletes become self-critical and negative, the zone is lost. Confidence is the key, and positive, helpful thoughts tend to keep confidence high.

3) <u>Use a Good Ritual:</u> It is rare to zone throughout an entire competition. Athletes who have done it manage their down-times extremely well. Most every sport has lapses in action. During these times, successful athletes control their eyes, stay relaxed, visualize ideal strategies, and remain present to their thoughts. These rituals must be practiced so they too become automatic. For more ideas on rituals, see Appendix D.

4) "Flash" Visualize: Just as you're about to execute a skill, imagine it in it's ideal form. Some examples include: Imagining where the ball will go on a tennis passing shot just prior to contact; Imagining the trajectory of a jump shot just prior to shooting; Imagining a move during a gymnastics floor routine just prior to executing it; Imagining a one-on-one move in basketball just prior to doing it. Great athletes get a flash image of what they are going to do, and then they simply copy what they have just seen in their mind. This kind of visualizing can and must be practiced regularly before it will work consistently in competition.

## Trying Without Caring

One might think "trying" and "caring" are both necessary for top performance, since few would try if they didn't care. However, we define "trying" and "caring" a little differently and believe that they CANNOT both be present in athletes DURING zone performances. Here's why. Trying reflects the amount of physical and mental effort put forth during competition. Trying is obviously important to every athlete and coach. However, the word "care" is defined by Webster's Dictionary as "to wish for or want" pertaining to a specific future outcome. Future thinking during competition is what creates nervousness. So caring about the outcome or what people might think DESTROYS the chance of zoning! Most athletes we meet can't imagine competing without caring about the outcome. They really struggle with letting go and being 'ok' with whatever the result ends up being. Here's a sentence we have our tennis player clients memorize in an attempt to help them with this issue: **"As long as I hustle for every ball, stay calm between points, and problem solve throughout the match, I know I'm doing everything I can in the moment and the score will be what it is."** We suggest creating a sentence like this that is specific to your sport or activity.

What we know about athletes in the zone is that they are so wrapped up in the moment, so focused on performance, that they are not consciously aware of consequences. In other words, in the moment of performing their skill, they do not "care" about what might or might not happen. Are they giving everything they have? Definitely! They may think about winning during breaks in action, but during the performance, in the middle of a zone experience, athletes simply don't care what might happen! So how do athletes get to this place of trying without caring?

Fortunately for all of us humans, we can only think of one thing at a time. That fact is what will save us all from underperforming or choking in our next big competition. All we have to do is recognize the future thought (usually a sentence starting with "What if...") and insert another thought or picture! This simple solution is not always easy, especially if you are emotional or have a habit of 'trying not to blow it' when things get tight. The key is to create a new habit of recognizing the future thought and exchanging it for a present thought.

What does it look like when someone is trying hard but doesn't care about the outcome? This might be someone who isn't 'supposed' to win, someone who has no expectations of what 'should' happen, someone who just really loves competition (and just enjoys participating), or someone who is focused on overcoming a mild injury (many people play their best when their thoughts are on how to get through a little pain!). Whatever the example, it usually looks GREAT! The person is sharp, focused, relaxed, smiles often, is clearly having a good time, and usually is performing their best!

Here are some ideas on how to achieve this 'trying without caring' state of mind:

1) Recognize Future Thoughts: Future thoughts are the ones that create importance and hence pressure. If these thoughts know they're not welcome, they won't come around too often! In order to get rid of them, you just have to consistently exchange them for strategy thoughts.

2) Smile Often: Enjoy the experience. Not only will it feel better, but you'll perform better. As the Chinese proverb goes, "Happiness is not a state to arrive at, but a manner of traveling."

3) Act As If: Do what people who LOVE to compete would do. They'd lay it all on the line and courageously battle throughout. They'd go for their shots. See Appendix F for more on who champions are.

37

4) <u>Play Like an Underdog</u>: Underdogs don't choke - they usually raise their level of play. Choose to do all the things an underdog does.

5) <u>It Is What It Is</u>: Look at occurrences for what they actually are, not what you THINK they are. A double fault in tennis doesn't mean you're serving terribly. It simply means you missed 2 serves in a row. Move on after mistakes without attaching 'meaning' that might stir up emotions.

The following interview with a professional tennis player is an example of what can happen when an athlete cares less about the outcome during competition. This athlete became so frustrated that at one point he said to himself, "Forget this tournament." But he's so passionate about the game that he couldn't stop trying even though he chose not to care any more about the outcome. The result? Trying without caring enabled him to play better and actually win the match.

---

May 25, 2004

PARIS (AP) -- Vince Spadea's comeback started when he stopped caring about winning. The American overcame nine match points and a 5-1 deficit in the fifth set Monday to beat French qualifier Florent Serra  7-5, 1-6, 4-6, 7-6 (7), 9-7.

Spadea said he began taking risky swings when he found himself on the verge of defeat. "I was like, just give it away. Forget this tournament," he said. "And everything went in."

Serra held so many match points in the 4 1/2 hour marathon that Spadea lost track. "I think he had about five or six," Spadea said. Instead, Spadea survived one match point trailing 7-6 in the tiebreaker. He overcame three serving at 5-3 in the final set, then erased five more in the next game to make the score 5-all.

Spadea, seeded 27th, converted his first match-point chance. "I'm a passionate guy about what I'm trying to accomplish," he said. "I just couldn't give up."

---

NOTE: If you're NOT trying AND don't care, you may be burned out (overtrained)! See Appendix C for information on how to recognize and treat overtraining.

## A New Model of How to Find the Zone During Performance

The "flow diagram" on the next page shows the process by which athletes can learn to control their emotions and find the zone <u>while they compete</u>. The letters below refer to the letters in the diagram:

(A) The process begins when the score gets close or when an athlete is trying to finish a competition.

(B) The tendency is for the athlete to go to the future and think about the possible outcome (what might happen).

(C) If that happens, the athlete will likely feel nervous, tight and/or conservative. This type of feeling typically leads to errors and poor decisions.

(D) If too many errors occur, thoughts tend to stay in the past.

(E) Past thoughts trigger anger, frustration or sadness.

At any of these 5 stages, the solution is the same - to 'GET PRESENT' by simply recognizing the feeling, thought or situation. The ideal path is from (A) to ' Recognize Situation' to 'Get Present' so nervousness and anger doesn't have to be experienced at all. Once present, the athlete can then breathe and relax, visualize an ideal strategy, use optimistic self-talk and try without caring about the outcome. The success wheel begins to spin (The ZONE). The Zone stops when thoughts venture outside the circle. By memorizing this Emotion Wheel, athletes can learn to consciously enhance their performance during competition.

## The Emotion Wheel

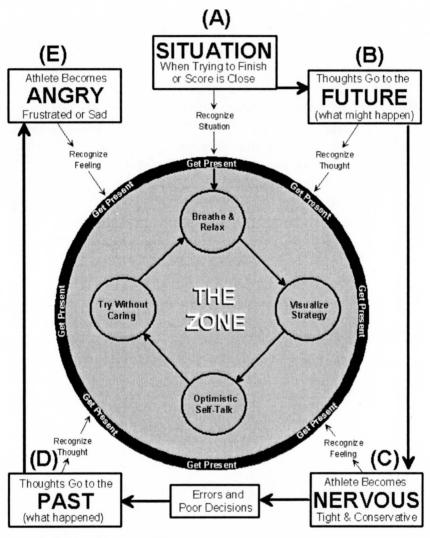

© 2004, Robert S. Neff

**Do This Exercise** (You'll use it later in Chapter 5)

Describe a zone experience you've had in the past. Start by giving it a title like "U.S. Open 2nd round." This title will serve to jog your mind. Attach your opponent's name if appropriate. Describe how you felt during the zone. Talk about your confidence level, your emotions, your energy level, how you handled mistakes, and how long the zone lasted. Describe your state of being, whether you were aggressive or passive, loud or quiet, fast walking or slow, and tight or loose. List any significant things you did to prepare that may have created this great performance. List any other things that you know consistently help you to find the zone.

Title: _____

How I Felt:

My Confidence, Emotions and Energy:

My Behavior and State of Being:

How I Should Prepare:

# Chapter 5:
# A Customized Mental Skills Training Program

*"In golf as in life, it is the follow through that makes the difference." Proverb*

## Follow-Through

This is the "follow through" chapter! When you finish it, you will have created your own mental skills training program consisting of concepts covered in this book. You will be able to use this program to incorporate what you've learned into your training regimen.

When we take on new sport psychology clients, we always custom design each program to fit the needs of the client. With that said, every client sets goals, learns to visualize, learns to control self-talk, and understands how emotions can affect their performance. However, each program is different because each client has different goals, different motivations, and different strengths and weaknesses (additionally, we may address other personal issues such as coach or parent conflicts, weight loss, diet issues, etc. that obviously cannot be covered in this book). This book was designed to be the next best thing to meeting with a sport psychologist 1-on-1.

## IMPORTANT!

Before you continue working in this chapter, be sure you have read the prior chapters and completed the exercises in each. Of particular importance are the 2 goal setting worksheets and the "Roadmap" sheet in Chapter 1.

Also, if you've skipped a "**Do This Exercise**" at the end of any of the chapters, go back now and finish them. We'll use the results of those exercises in the next section.

When you're ready, come back here and continue...

## The 7 Steps

**Step 1:** Post your "Roadmap" goalsheet from Chapter 1 in a visible place where you will see it each day (on the wall in your room, on the mirror of your bathroom, in your car...). If you completed it with thought and care, it will continually motivate and direct you. You will want to update your Roadmap every 60 days. Put today's date on it and write the date 60 days from now in the "Update By" area at the bottom of your Roadmap.

**Step 2:** You will now begin filling out a "Monitoring Chart" that will help you keep track of the activities you plan to do each week to improve your mental skills. Go a few pages ahead and take a look at it, then come back here and follow the steps below. Each week, you will be able to print additional charts at our website: http://www.roadmaptothezone.com.

**Step 3:** Take out the goal setting exercise you did at the end of Chapter 1. On the monitoring chart, write the "Next Major Roadmap Goal" and then list the "5 Action Goals" you plan to do to reach your Roadmap goal (in the future, you will create a list of action goals similar to this for whatever the next major goal becomes).

**Step 4:** The blank table on the monitoring chart will be used to track the mental skills you choose to practice each week. We suggest to our new clients that each of the following be listed for at least the first month:

1) <u>Visualize</u>: Use the sequences you wrote in the Chapter 2 exercise, but you may also want to use the other lists included in Chapter 2. We recommend you visualize for at least a few minutes each day;

2) <u>Read or contribute to your "Zone Log"</u>: List this in the table so you'll remember to add all your best performances to the log;

3) <u>Read a Biography:</u> Learn about the best athletes in your sport. List which biography you've chosen and how often you'll read. We recommend several times a week;

4) <u>Watch Pros Perform</u>: Watch the best in your sport perform. Note how often you will do this. We recommend several times a week;

5) <u>Watch video of yourself performing</u>: You know what you want to look like when performing. Critique yourself weekly. See Appendix G for a form you can use to evaluate your mental skills after a competition;

6) <u>Analyze self-talk</u>: After each competition, list the thoughts you had while competing, label them as in Chapter 3.

**Step 5**: Take out the visualization exercise you did at the end of Chapter 2. On the monitoring chart, list the 3 sequences or actions you need to improve or that you need to execute to perform well. This is what you will visualize each day.

**Step 6**: Take out the self-talk exercise you did at the end of Chapter 3. In the boxes on the monitoring chart, write any harmful thoughts you are committing to give up, and then write several helpful thoughts you will use instead.

**Step 7**: The last box on the monitoring chart is a place for you to quickly note zone performances that may occur during the week. Take out the zone exercise you did at the end of Chapter 4. You are going to create a "Zone Log" where you record all your great performances. You will be able to read this log before competitions to overcome nervousness, any time you have low confidence, or when you are in a performance slump. The Chapter 4 exercise you did can be your first entry. We recommend using a small spiral notebook that you can carry with you to your competitions.

**Mental Skills Monitoring Chart**          **Beginning:** ___/___/___

**Next Major "Roadmap" Goal:** _____

**Action Goals for This Week:**

1)
2)
3)
4)
5)

| Activities | Goal | Mon | Tue | Wed | Thu | Fri | Sat | Sun | Done |
|------------|------|-----|-----|-----|-----|-----|-----|-----|------|
|            |      |     |     |     |     |     |     |     |      |
|            |      |     |     |     |     |     |     |     |      |
|            |      |     |     |     |     |     |     |     |      |
|            |      |     |     |     |     |     |     |     |      |
|            |      |     |     |     |     |     |     |     |      |
|            |      |     |     |     |     |     |     |     |      |
|            |      |     |     |     |     |     |     |     |      |
| Check the far right column when the goal is completed for the week. | | | | | | | | | |

**Visualization Sequences** (sit in a quiet place, imagine doing them perfectly)

1)
2)
3)

| Harmful Thoughts I'm Giving Up | Helpful Thoughts I'll Begin Using |
|-------------------------------|-----------------------------------|
| | |
| **New Performances for My Zone Log** | |
| | |

Additional, full size, charts can be printed from: http://www.roadmaptothezone.com

## Journey's End

We hope the information in this book has been helpful and inspiring as you journey toward your highest performance dreams. As with all 'self-help' books, the information presented is only really beneficial if it is incorporated into day-to-day routines.

To assist you with using this information, we have created a special website for those who purchased this book. To access this site, you will need the username and password found at the bottom of Appendix E in this book.

Go to http://www.roadmaptothezone.com and click on the MEMBER SITE link.

We wish you all the success you deserve.

Enjoy the inspirational stories we've included right after the Appendices.

.

*"It is good to have an end to journey toward, but it is the journey that matters in the end."* -Ursula LeGuin

# Appendices

# Appendix A: Progressive Relaxation

Prior to beginning your progressive relaxation routine, have someone whose voice you find pleasant tape record the text below. Tell that person to speak slowly and clearly, pausing to give you time to respond.

---

**Directions**: Turn on the tape and follow the script.

*Lie down or sit in a comfortable position. I'm going to ask you to tense and relax various parts of your body. When I say TENSE, I'd like you to tense that body part. I'll then say, "and.... RELAX." When I say "and..." you should take in a deep breath. When I say, "RELAX' you should exhale and let go of all tension. Ideally, you're looking to connect your deep breathes with muscle relaxation.*

*Get in touch with your breathing. Breathe out, breathe in. Imagine that as each body part is relaxed, all tension leaves.*

*TENSE your toes. Hold it, feel it, AND... RELAX.*
*TENSE your ankles and calves. Hold it, feel it, AND... RELAX..*
*TENSE your thighs. Hold it, feel it, AND... RELAX.*
*Remember to breathe slowly and deeply.*

*TENSE your buttocks. Hold it, feel it, AND... RELAX.*
*PRESS your lower back against the floor. Hold it, feel it, AND... RELAX.*
*TENSE your stomach. Hold it, feel it, AND... RELAX.*
*PULL your shoulders back. Hold it, feel it, AND... RELAX.*
*Push your shoulders forward. Hold it, feel it, AND... RELAX.*

Make a fist with your hands. Hold it, feel it, AND... RELAX.
TENSE the muscles in your arms. Hold it, feel it, AND...
RELAX.

Now let's work on your face and head.
Clench your jaw. Hold it, feel it, AND... RELAX..
Open your mouth wide. Hold it, feel it, AND... RELAX.
Scrunch up your whole face. Hold it, feel it, AND... RELAX.
Eyes closed. Just RELAX.
When you open your eyes, you will feel refreshed and
ready to take on whatever life brings to you.

## Appendix B: Cognitive Relaxation

(another way to relax!)

## Directions:

The following relaxation sequence is designed to help you relax your muscles so you'll be able to find the right muscle tension during competition. This sequence should be practiced 3 to 4 times per week for several weeks before consistent control is attained. Once control is attained, practice regularly each month to maintain it.

For best results, read the following script out loud and record onto an audio tape (or have a person with a more pleasant voice do it). Then play back the audio tape when practicing relaxation.

-----------------------------------------------------------------

"Find a comfortable position where you'll be able to relax ALL your muscles and close your eyes. Try to get as relaxed as you can for today. If you're not completely relaxed, that's OK for now. Finish up whatever is on your mind and then focus on the feeling of the air going in and out of your nose.

Now, imagine a strong, warm beam of light shining on your forehead and sending penetrating waves of warm relaxation into your scalp - smoothing out all the wrinkles. This beam of light might feel like the sun shining down on you, but narrow like a flashlight beam. These waves are slowly spreading out over your eyelids and penetrating into your eyes - making your eyes feel soft and warm.

You are feeling more and more relaxed as the waves spread further down your face to your nose and cheeks. The warm waves of relaxation moving further down to your mouth and jaw. Your lips may part slightly as the rest of the muscles in your face become completely relaxed, not a wrinkle to be found.

These warm penetrating waves now move down your neck and into your shoulders and upper back. Feel the warm relaxation loosening any tight areas and you notice how much better you are beginning to feel. These waves that are coming from the warm beam of light still shining on your forehead are now penetrating deep into your biceps and triceps, and now into your forearm, massaging, soothing and relaxing.

As the warm waves now move over your wrists and into your hands, you might feel a tingling in your fingers, relaxing you further and further, deeper and deeper. With each exhale your become more relaxed. These waves of relaxation now move out over your chest and back and down through your stomach and waste - a warm penetrating wavy calm.

These waves now move through your hips and lower back and into your butt and upper legs. Feel your thigh muscles just shut off as your legs begin to feel heavy. These warm penetrating waves of relaxation now approach your knees and then into your shins and calves. Your legs may feel like they're melting into the floor/carpet/bed as your relaxation becomes deeper and deeper. Finally the waves reach your ankles, feet and toes. You feel peaceful and relaxed from head to toe; you are secure and happy that you feel as good as you do.

Now, as I count backward from 5 to 1, you will begin to energize. When I reach "1" you'll feel relaxed and refreshed. 5-4-3-2-1. When you feel like it, just open your eyes. Feel energized and confident that relaxation practice like this will make you a better athlete by allowing you to control excess muscle tension. To relax during competition, just breathe deeply and think of the beam of light sending waves of relaxation into any tight muscles."

## Appendix C: Athletic Burnout

(the opposite of being in the zone!)

**Physical Signs:** Feelings of exhaustion, a lingering cold, frequent gastrointestinal problems (stomach aches), frequent headaches, sleeplessness, shortness of breath and strange weight loss are examples.

**Behavioral Signs:** Quick temper, instantaneous frustration, feeling overburdened (first thought of the day is "Oh, no!"), inability to hold feelings in, yelling and screaming, feelings of helplessness, giving up easily, loss of caring for loved ones, greater risk taking behavior and consistently decreased performances are examples.

**Sport Related Signs:** Reduced feel for the skill or movement, never happy with performance, start to expect bad performance, slower reactions, increased unforced errors over many competitions, difficulty focusing (poor concentration/eye control), treat coach and teammates like strangers and general impatience are examples.

**Ideal Candidate for Burnout:** A dedicated, overachiever with an external locus of control (does things for other people or for extrinsic rewards) or a person with extreme role conflict or role ambiguity (doesn't understand herself or how she fits into a variety of situations) [Fender (1989), Athlete burnout, <u>The Sport Psychologist</u>, 3 (1), pp. 63-71].

## Burnout Avoidance

1) Become more aware of the symptoms and underlying causes of each;

2) Cross training (use other related sports to help accomplish fitness goals);

3) Day(s) off (proper "periodization training" should include days off);

4) Change of scenery (different practice location, inside vs. outside, road trips);

5) Support from others (friends, family, coach, sport psychologist);

6) Work with a sport psychologist;

7) Tournament scheduling (allow time to rest and recover);

8) Practice scheduling (quality not just quantity);

9) Proper goal setting (focus only on things you control).

## Appendix D: More Information About Rituals

*"Rituals: Establish rituals during competition and down-times to appropriately balance relaxation, focus and intensity."* Dr. Jim Loehr

**Importance:** Everyone depends on rituals as they go through their lives. Rituals free us up to think about more important tasks. If you think about it, each of us has literally hundreds of rituals we use each day, without even knowing it. From tying shoe laces, to walking to writing and driving a car - they're all habits that we had to think about at first but now they're automatic. Accomplished athletes depend on rituals as well. Every stroke you have as a tennis player or golfer as well as how you move around the court, field, track, rink, etc. are all rituals. Usually, the more consistent the ritual, the better the athlete. One of the most important mental habits is something called a Refocus Ritual (RR). It simply represents an ideal way to spend your down time so you're as ready as you can be to start competing when play starts again. Think about all the down time in golf between shots, tennis between points, football between plays, baseball between pitches, etc. Our research shows that athletes with strong mental skills use an RR similar to the one described in the next section.

**How To Practice:** Because every sport has different demands, athletes obviously make modifications to suit their needs. Here's the RR that most experienced tennis players with strong mental skills use. As soon as the point ends, players: 1) Turn away from their opponent and switch their racket to their non-dominant hand (to relax arm). They usually hold the racket by the throat so the racket head is up (instead of by the handle with the racket head down); 2) Control their eyes by keeping them first on the ground, then on their strings and then on opponent (thus reducing distractions); 3) Breathe and relaxe muscles by lowering shoulders and shaking out arms and legs; and 4) Visualize how they plan to start the next point. When said all in sequence, it rhymes: "Switch the racket - Control the eyes - Breathe-relax - and Visualize." Just like any habit, athletes have to think about it every time they practice, at least for the first 3-4 weeks, until it becomes an unconscious ritual.

**Note:** Not all accomplished athletes use exactly the same ritual. However, when athletes are in the zone and have to deal with down time, they all do very similar things involving relaxation, eye control, positive self-talk and visualization.

# Appendix E: Making Practice More Like Competition

**When Preparing to Practice:** <u>Come early, ready to work (just like in competition):</u>

1) Have equipment pre-packed and ready to go;
2) Bring a towel, ace bandages and an empty ice bag;
3) Bring a change of clothes;
4) Bring your training journal or logbook;
5) Bring some energy bars;
6) Anything else you think is important to your performance.

**When Practicing:** <u>Set mini goals for yourself using the following ideas:</u>

1) Time (Example: Hit cross court forehands for 10 minutes);
2) Number in a row (Example: Hit 25 wedge shots in a row);
3) Number out of 10 (Example: Make 9 out of 10 free throws);
4) Total number (Example: Throw 100 pitches per day, 3 times a week);
5) Use a target area (Example: Hit all forehands cross court past the service line);
6) Certain score (Example: Shoot under 35 on the back 9 holes).

**When Simulating Competition** (practice matches, scrimmages, etc.)

<u>Real competition has one thing that most practice situations don't have - CONSEQUENCES.</u> To excel when it really

counts, you must be able to put consequences aside and perform. The only way to do that is to practice performing with consequences present! Therefore, create a meaningful consequence for the outcome every time you compete. Be creative. Some ideas include:

1) Fitness (jump rope; wall-sits; lunges; crunches; pushups; agility sprints; super squat thrusts; mile run; etc.). Since fitness is beneficial, perhaps the winner should get to do it!

2) Loser services the winner (carry bags for a day; washes car; cleans inside of car; buys a drink; buys lunch; does laundry; etc.);

3) Winner avoids something unpleasant (no clean-up; better room when traveling; traveling 1st class; extra day of rest, etc.).

User: athlete   Pwd: athlete

## Appendix F: Who Champions Are

Of these 30 qualities, how many do you 'own'? Ask some-one who really knows you as an athlete to rate you on each of these (from 0 to 10). A score of 250 or more is awesome, 150-250 is OK, and less than 150 is poor. Work to improve these qualities.

| Quality | Your Rating 0 (low) to 10 (high) |
| --- | --- |
| self-disciplined | |
| determined | |
| a hard worker | |
| persistent (doesn't quit) | |
| dedicated (committed) | |
| has 'heart' | |
| loves the sport | |
| self-confident | |
| sets high goals | |
| has 'guts' (no fear) | |
| loves competition | |
| motivated | |
| strong character (ethics) | |
| respects opponent | |
| appreciative | |
| patient | |
| coachable | |
| classy (as in a 'class act') | |
| optimistic (sees good future) | |
| positive | |
| tenacious (fight) | |
| aggressive | |
| organized (manages time) | |
| focused | |
| passionate | |
| humble (doesn't brag) | |
| gracious (good winner) | |
| detail oriented (not sloppy) | |
| improvement oriented | |
| thankful | |
| **Total (out of 300)** | |

## Appendix G: Mental Skills Evaluation

Complete this form after each competition. Keep as a reminder of lessons learned.

| Name: | Date: |
|-------|-------|
| Opponent: | |

| Skills | Poor or Low | | OK | Great or High | |
|--------|------|---|-----|------|---|
| Overall attitude ................................... | 1 | 2 | 3 | 4 | 5 |
| Ability to refocus after distractions.............. | 1 | 2 | 3 | 4 | 5 |
| Physical effort ................................... | 1 | 2 | 3 | 4 | 5 |
| Sportsmanship ................................... | 1 | 2 | 3 | 4 | 5 |
| Problem solving .......... ...................... | 1 | 2 | 3 | 4 | 5 |
| Use of ideal rituals................................ | 1 | 2 | 3 | 4 | 5 |
| Ideal muscle tension.............................. | 1 | 2 | 3 | 4 | 5 |
| Ability to avoid getting angry..................... | 1 | 2 | 3 | 4 | 5 |
| Ability to avoid getting nervous.................. | 1 | 2 | 3 | 4 | 5 |
| Ability to get into the ZONE and stay there for extended periods of time......................... | 1 | 2 | 3 | 4 | 5 |
| **Total Points** | | | **/50** | | |

## Key Areas to Improve:

1.


2.


3.

## Appendix H: Chiropractic Health Care for Athletes

Where does an athlete, whether professional, semiprofessional, high school or weekend warrior, go when a sports injury occurs? Frequently, the normal response is to first go to one's family, general or internal medicine practitioner. If the response to treatment is unsuccessful, a referral to an orthopedic surgeon is likely the next step. This approach may be fine, unless the injury is to the athlete's spine or an extremity joint.

Chiropractors are primary health care providers skilled to diagnose and treat neuromusculoskeletal disorders, which encompass the nervous, muscular and skeletal systems. The musculoskeletal system is the region of the body which encounters the majority of athletic injuries due to acute trauma and/or overuse.

Sporting injuries usually result in injury to the muscles, tendons, joints, ligaments, bone and discs, all of which a chiropractor can properly diagnose, and in most cases treat. So how are these injuries treated? Treatment at a chiropractor's office will probably include spinal and/or extremity (shoulder, elbow, wrist, hip, knee, ankle) manipulations or "adjustments" or mobilization techniques depending on the injury. Adjustments are usually necessary due to spinal fixations, or abnormal motioning vertebrae and/or other joints caused by trauma, accidents, emotional stress, degenerative changes or chemical imbalances. Adjustments unlock the fixated joint, which in turn allows the muscles to relax and balance. They also increase the blood flow and decrease nerve irritation surrounding the joint which creates normal healing for the adjacent muscles and other body tissues. This is vitally necessary for proper functioning of the body, and to prevent further injury on the playing field. In conjunction, physical therapy modalities, specific stretching and active rehabilitative exercises are prescribed. Nutritional advice is also given when necessary. At times, outside diagnostic tests for CT, MRI, EMG, etc. may be necessary and or medical referrals to other specialists depending on the severity of the condition. In general, effective chiropractors are usually excellent teachers. A key component that can enable athletes to recover quickly and to decrease further injuries is knowledge of the human body. Successful athletes are often 'students of the game' and very well read in areas such as biomechanics and health science. Chiropractors can be an excellent source of training and prevention information.

Fortunately, athletes of all ages and sports have found great relief and lasting benefits from chiropractic care. Also, having a chiropractor as part of a multidisciplinary health team for more complex injuries is prudent. Recently, there has been an acute awareness of the benefits associated with receiving chiropractic treatment to recover faster and more effectively from injury, to prevent further injuries, and to obtain optimal results in specific sporting activities.

Chiropractors have been evaluating and treating athletes since the early 1900s. Baseball great Babe Ruth was a chiropractic patient. Today chiropractors serve as members of the US Olympic health care team and are usually the most sought after doctor for the athletes. Chiropractors also serve as part of the health care team for the Pan American games, numerous professional, collegiate and high school football, baseball and basketball teams, pro rodeo, pro beach volleyball, bodybuilding, cycling competitions, pro water polo, USA track and field events, PGA golfers and for many tennis professionals.

The list of professional athletes who have used chiropractic care during their careers is an impressive one. Some of the more well-known ones include tennis stars Andre Agassi, Ivan Lendl and Billy Jean King; cyclist and Tour de

France champion Lance Armstrong; baseball's new home run leader Barry Bonds and former home run champion Mark McGuire; golfers Tiger Woods and Chi Chi Rodriguez; boxer Evander Holyfield; football players Troy Aikman, Emmitt Smith and Joe Montana; basketball players Charles Barkley, Karl Malone and John Stockton; volleyball pro Karch Kiraldy; World Olympic decathlon champion Dan O'Brien; World 100 meter sprint champion Donovan Baily; and US Top 1500 meter runner Regina Jacobs. Some of the above mentioned athletes believe so strongly in regular chiropractic care that they actually fly their personal chiropractor with them for their particular sporting event.

Chiropractic education following undergraduate college education involves four years of studying including anatomy, physiology, neuroanatomy, radiology, biochemistry, pediatrics, gerontology, nutrition, biomechanics, physiotherapy, differential diagnoses, adjusting technique courses, exercise, rehabilitation, etc. In conjunction, there is one year of clinical internship. Stringent State and National Board examinations must be passed prior to becoming licensed to practice chiropractic medicine.

Chiropractors believe in the innate healing qualities of the human body, particularly when the right approach to treatment of a disorder is applied. In conjunction, many believe that there are three stages of proper treatment following an injury: 1) The relief stage, or the time necessary for the individual to get out of pain; 2) The healing stage, or the time it takes for the body to be at 100% or close to it, the time for tissues to heal properly, and for the individual to return to their particular sport; and, 3) The maintenance stage, which represents a time when the athlete may choose to come in periodically to prevent further injuries and to allow the body to perform to its potential. Many athletes visit chiropractors not necessarily just because of a new injury, but for preventative medicine as well.

This philosophy of chiropractic care and its treatment approach appears to correspond well with the attitude of the athlete, particularly the elite athlete. For elite athletes to achieve top performance, they need properly functioning nervous and musculoskeletal systems as well as efficient biomechanics. The chiropractor's role as part of the performance health care team is essential for most athletes to achieve their goals.

*Dr. Glen Silver assisted with the above article and comes strongly recommended by Dr. Robert Neff. Dr. Silver has been in private practice since 1990 and currently owns and operates two multidisciplinary and multifaceted health care centers in Dallas, Texas. He routinely treats sports injuries for athletes of all ages. Dr. Silver can be contacted at 214-942-1212*

# Inspirational Stories

Inspiration comes in many ways and from many sources. We hope you are first motivated internally, perhaps by a voice or drive to excel. We also hope you have positive, supportive people around you to guide and encourage you. This section is a collection of real-life stories that will inspire and motivate you to go on when you think you can't, believe when you probably shouldn't, and look deep inside yourself for the greatness we know lies there. We hope the stories make a lasting impression and that you enjoy reading them.

## Diving for Gold

In the 10 meter diving competition, the lone American, Laura Wilkinson (a TEXAS girl!), was not faring all that well. Her 2nd dive out of 5 had her placed # 8, behind a pair of consistent, mechanical Chinese competitors and a pair of equally tough Canadian competitors.

Her 3rd dive took her to # 5 -- and the commentators made note that she would at least have a very slim chance at winning the Bronze Medal -- verrrrrrry slim. They went on to talk about the fact that Laura Wilkinson even being in Sydney was a miracle. Earlier in the year, Laura Wilkinson broke 3 tiny bones in her foot, making practice absolutely impossible for 6 months. At 22 years of age, her goal, her dream, her entire focus had been on qualifying for the 2000 Olympics. It looked as though that dream had been dashed.

However, rather than give up, instead of physically practicing her dives, Laura spent countless hours, days and months VISUALIZING her dives. She watched herself on the platform, setting herself, pushing off and diving through the air, completing series of mid-air, grueling acrobatics and, finally, gliding, seemingly effortlessly, into the water. She practiced day after day in her mind, all the while keeping a positive attitude. And, she saw the job through. In her mind, she would visualize herself winning the Gold . . . on the platform, medal around her neck, the American Flag being raised to the strains of the Star Spangled Banner, tears flowing, bright smile covering wet cheeks.

Dive #3 -- AWESOME! Beautiful, as close to perfect as possible without nailing it!!! WOW!!! But, it would never be enough to unseat those ahead of her, especially the Chinese who had been trained since early childhood in all the arts that comprise the dive. They were little machines, never flinching, always consistent. Laura Wilkinson, after all, had only taken up diving 6 years before. Her positive attitude and infectious smile were what the commentators continued to talk about as, one after another, the numbers 1, 2, 3 and 4 competitors took their turns completing beautiful, methodical dives. There was no way under Heaven that Laura Wilkinson had any chance of accomplishing her goal -- taking home that Gold Medal. But, oh what a great job she had done hanging in there! And through it all, every time the camera caught her, there she was, smiling brightly, holding on to that positive attitude.

Dive #4 -- AWESOME!!! Another beautiful, near-perfect dive. WOW!!!!! But, it would take serious mistakes on the parts of every single one of the 4 competitors placed above her to enable her to have any real hope of winning the gold -- and at least 3 of the 4 didn't make mistakes. Then the most incredible thing happened . . . . one after another, each of the top 4 fell, each fall caused by miscalculations that seemed impossible just moments before.

Before the 5th and final dive, Laura Wilkinson was in the #1 position -- but could she hold it? There she was, smiling brightly, eyes shining, at the top of the platform. Beaming over to her parents, letting them know through her eyes and her smile, heart-to-heart, how much she loved them. Instead of showing the enormous pressure any other person would have felt under the circumstances, she stood . . . glowing. As she took in every cheer, every flash, her eyes shone, her smile beamed, her heart was full. She stood there for a few moments, basking in the warmth.

Then, she moved to her position on the platform . . . set her body, her eyes, her mind . . and dove for the last time in this event. Another near-perfect dive. Again, her competition could not withstand the pressure. Again, one after another, they failed to be able to catch her.

Her dream had been realized. Laura Wilkinson had won the Gold.

## Shake It Off and Step Up

A parable is told of a farmer who owned an old mule. A mule fell into a farmer's well. The farmer heard the mule 'braying' --or-- whatever mules do when they fall into wells. After carefully assessing the situation, the farmer sympathized with the mule, but decided that neither the mule nor the well was worth the trouble of saving. Instead, he called his neighbors together and told them what had happened... and enlisted them to help haul dirt to bury the old mule in the well and put him out of his misery.

Initially, the old mule was hysterical! But as the farmer and his neighbors continued shoveling and the dirt hit his back...a thought struck him. It suddenly dawned on him that every time a shovel load of dirt landed on his back...HE SHOULD SHAKE IT OFF AND STEP UP! This he did, blow after blow. "Shake it off and step up...shake it off and step up... shake it off and step up!" he repeated to encourage himself. No matter how painful the blows, or distressing the situation seemed the old mule fought "panic" and just kept right on SHAKING IT OFF AND STEPPING UP! You're right! It wasn't long before the old mule, battered and exhausted, STEPPED TRIUMPHANTLY OVER THE WALL OF THAT WELL! What seemed like it would bury him, actually blessed him...all because of the manner in which he handled his adversity.

THAT'S LIFE! If we face our problems and respond to them positively, and refuse to give in to panic, bitterness, or self-pity...THE ADVERSITIES THAT COME ALONG TO BURY US USUALLY HAVE WITHIN THEM THE POTENTIAL TO BENEFIT AND BLESS US! Remember that FORGIVENESS--FAITH--PRAYER-- PRAISE and HOPE...all are excellent ways to "SHAKE IT OFF AND STEP UP" out of the wells in which we find ourselves!

## Struggles with Difficulties

In midst of your struggle with difficulties, remember this story.

A man found a cocoon of a butterfly. One day a small opening appeared, he sat and watched the butterfly for several hours as it struggled to force its body through that little hole. Then it seemed to stop making any progress. It appeared as if it had gotten as far as it could and it could go no farther. So the man decided to help the butterfly, he took a pair of scissors and snipped off the remaining bit of the cocoon. The butterfly then emerged easily. But it had a swollen body and small, shriveled wings. The man continued to watch the butterfly because he expected that, at any moment, the wings would enlarge and expand to be able to support the body, which would contract in time. Neither happened! In fact, the butterfly spent the rest of its life crawling around with a swollen body and shriveled wings. It never was able to fly.

What the man in his kindness and haste did not understand was that the restricting cocoon and the struggle required for the butterfly to get through the tiny opening were Nature's way of forcing fluid from the body of the butterfly into its wings so that it would be ready for flight once it achieved its freedom from the cocoon.

Sometimes struggles are exactly what we need in our life. If God allowed us to go through our life without any obstacles, it would cripple us. We would not be as strong as what we could have been. And we could never fly. So have a nice day and struggle a little. You might find something can be gained from it!

## The Joy Is In The Journey

Far too often, achieving what you set out to do is not the important thing.

Two young brothers decided to dig a deep hole behind their house. As they were working, a couple of older boys stopped by to watch. "What are you doing?" asked one of the visitors. "We plan to dig a hole all the way through the earth!" one of the brothers volunteered excitedly.

The older boys began to laugh, telling the younger ones that digging a hole all the way through the earth was impossible. After a long silence, one of the young diggers picked up a jar full of spiders, worms and a wide assortment of insects. He removed the lid and showed the wonderful contents to the scoffing visitors.

Then he said quietly and confidently, "Even if we don't dig all the way through the earth, look what we found along the way!"

Their goal was far too ambitious, but it did cause them to dig. And that is what a goal is for - to cause us to move in the direction we have chosen; in other words, to set us to digging!

But not every goal will be fully achieved. Not every job will end successfully. Not every relationship will endure. Not every hope will come to pass. Not every love will last. Not every endeavor will be completed. Not every dream will be realized.

But when you fall short of your aim, perhaps you can say, "Yes, but look at what I found along the way! Look at the wonderful things which have come into my life because I tried to do something!"

## Keep Your Goals in Sight

When she looked ahead, Florence Chadwick saw nothing but a solid wall of fog. Her body was numb. She had been swimming for nearly sixteen hours.

Already she was the first woman to swim the English Channel in both directions. Now, at age 34, her goal was to become the first woman to swim from Catalina Island to the California coast.

On that Fourth of July morning in 1952, the sea was like an ice bath and the fog was so dense she could hardly see her support boats. Sharks cruised toward her lone figure, only to be driven away by rifle shots. Against the frigid grip of the sea, she struggled on - hour after hour - while millions watched on national television.

Alongside Florence in one of the boats, her mother and her trainer offered encouragement. They told her it wasn't much farther. But all she could see was fog. They urged her not to quit. She never had . . . until then. With only a half mile to go, she asked to be pulled out.

Still thawing her chilled body several hours later, she told a reporter, "Look, I'm not excusing myself, but if I could have seen land I might have made it." It was not fatigue or even the cold water that defeated her. It was the fog. She was unable to see her goal.

Two months later, she tried again. This time, despite the same dense fog, she swam with her faith intact and her goal clearly pictured in her mind. She knew that somewhere be-hind that fog was land and this time she made it! Florence Chadwick became the first woman to swim the Catalina Channel, eclipsing the men's record by two hours!

## The Secret of Jimmy Yen, by Adam Khan

A jury of distinguished scholars and scientists, including Albert Einstein and Orville Wright thought enough of Jimmy Yen to vote him one of the top ten Modern Revolutionaries of the Twentieth Century. Yet all he did was teach Chinese peasants to read.

What made that so amazing was that for four thousand years reading and writing in China was only done by the Scholars. "Everybody" knew, including the peasants themselves, that peasants were incapable of learning.

That thoroughly ingrained cultural belief was Jimmy Yen's first impossible" barrier. The second barrier was the Chinese language itself, consisting of 40,000 characters, each character signifying a different word! The third barrier was the lack of technology and good roads. How could Jimmy Yen reach the 350 million peasants in China?

Impossible odds, an impossibly huge goal-and yet he had almost attained it when he was forced (by Communism) to leave his country.

Did he give up? No. He learned from defeat and expanded his goal: Teach the rest of the Third World to read. Practical reading programs, like the ones he invented in China, started pumping out literate people like a gushing oil well in the Philippines, Thailand, Sri Lanka, Nepal, Kenya, Columbia, Guatemala, Indonesia, Bangladesh, Ghana, India-people became literate. For the first time in their entire genetic history, they had access to the accumulated knowledge of the human race.

For those of us who take literacy for granted, I'd like you to consider for a moment how narrow your world would be if you'd never learned how to read and there was no access to radios or TVs.

180,000 Chinese peasants were hired by the Allied Forces in WW1 as laborers in the war effort. Most of them had no idea-not a clue-where England, Germany or France was, they didn't know what they were being hired to do, and didn't even know what a war was!

Try to grasp, if you will, the vacancy, the darkness, the lack that existed in those people because they couldn't read. Jimmy Yen was a savior to them.

What was the secret of Jimmy Yen's success? He found a real need, and found in himself a strong desire to answer that need. And he took some action: He tried to do something about it even though it seemed impossible. He worked long hours. And he started with what he had in front of him and gradually took on more and more, a little upon a little.

The English author Thomas Carlyle said, "Our main business is not to see what lies dimly at a distance, but to do what lies clearly at hand." And that's what Jimmy Yen did. He started out teaching a few peasants to read, with no desks, no pens, no money, no overhead projectors. He started from where he found himself and did what was clearly at hand.

And that's all you need to do. Start now. Start here. And do what lies clearly at hand.

**If Life is a Game, These Are the Rules**

Rule #1:

You will receive a body. Chances are, it won't be the body you would have ordered from the factory if you'd been given the opportunity. But as you grow older, you'll realize it's not only adequate for the job, it's phenomenal!

Rule #2:

You will be presented with lessons. And more times than not, these lessons will be an opportunity for you to decide whether to be a victim or victorious.

Rule #3:

There are no mistakes, only lessons.

Rule #4

Lessons are repeated until they're learned. What does it mean to "learn" a lesson? Embrace and internalize the lesson, actually accept it. And don't be surprised if that lesson comes back in different circumstances -- it may be asking, "Recognize me?"

Rule #5:

Learning does not end, for any of us. No matter how rich, thin or pretty someone may look to you, rest assured that they're learning lessons, too. That's the way of the world.

Rule #6:

"There" is no better than "here." Don't fall into the trap of "when I, then I." This rule is about being here with your circumstances, being happy, choosing to grow and not waiting until you get somewhere else before you enjoy your life.

Rule #7:

Others are only mirrors of you. Watch your judgments of people and things. Chances are, your judgments say more about you than what you're saying about someone else. Rather than judge, look below to the emotions that are fueling your desire to judge.

Rule #8:

What you make of life is up to you. It's your choice, all the way.

Rule #9:

All the answers lie inside you. And you can hear them, if you can find a still space inside yourself to listen. The noise of the world will drown out the voice of God -- your intuition -- if you let it.

Rule #10:

You have forgotten all of this at birth. Remembering and forgetting is the dance of consciousness. But guess what. If you listen to your intuition and pay attention to the lessons, you will remember these rules and be empowered to create your perfect life.

## You Have Two Choices

The following is a story with an important 'life lesson' to be learned. As always, 'life lessons' are extremely valuable when applied to sports.

Jerry was the kind of guy some people loved to hate. He was always in a good mood and always had something positive to say. When someone would ask him how he was doing, he would reply, "If I were any better, I would be twins!" He was a unique manager because he had several waiters who had followed him around from restaurant to restaurant. The reason the waiters followed Jerry was because of his attitude. He was a natural motivator. If an employee was having a bad day, Jerry was there telling the employee how to look on the positive side of the situation.

Seeing this style really made me curious, so one day I went up to Jerry and asked him, "I don't get it! You can't be a positive person all of the time. How do you do it?" Jerry replied, "Each morning I wake up and say to myself, Jerry, you have two choices today. You can choose to be in a good mood or you can choose to be in a bad mood.' I choose to be in a good mood. Each time something bad happens, I can choose to be a victim or I can choose to learn from it. I choose to learn from it.

Every time someone comes to me complaining, I can choose to accept their complaining or I can point out the positive side of life. I choose the positive side of life." "Yeah, right, it's not that easy," I protested. "Yes it is," Jerry said. "Life is all about choices. When you cut away all the junk, every situation is a choice. You choose how you react to situations.

You choose how people will affect your mood. You choose to be in a good mood or bad mood. The bottom line: It's your choice how you live life." I reflected on what Jerry said.

Soon thereafter, I left the restaurant industry to start my own business. We lost touch, but often thought about him when I made a choice about life instead of reacting to it. Several years later, I heard that Jerry did something you are never supposed to do in a restaurant business: he left the back door open one morning and was held up at gunpoint by three armed robbers. While trying to open the safe, his hand, shaking from nervousness, slipped off the combination. The robbers panicked and shot him. Luckily, Jerry was found relatively quickly and rushed to the local trauma center. After 18 hours of surgery and weeks of intensive care, Jerry was released from the hospital with fragments of the bullets still in his body.

I saw Jerry about six months after the accident. When I asked him how he was, he replied, "If I were any better, I'd be twins. Wanna see my scars?" I declined to see his wounds, but did ask him what had gone through his mind as the robbery took place.

"The first thing that went through my mind was that I should have locked the back door," Jerry replied. "Then, as I lay on the floor, I remembered that I had two choices: I could choose to live, or I could choose to die. I chose to live. "Weren't you scared? Did you lose consciousness?" I asked. Jerry continued, "The paramedics were great. They kept telling me I was going to be fine. But when they wheeled me into the emergency room and I saw the expressions on the faces of the doctors and nurses, I got really scared... In their eyes, I read, 'He's a dead man. " I knew I needed to take action." "What did you do?" I asked. "Well, there was a big, burly nurse shouting questions at me," said Jerry. "She asked if I was allergic to anything. 'Yes,' I replied.

The doctors and nurses stopped working as they waited for my reply. I took a deep breath and yelled, 'Bullets!' Over their laughter, I told them, 'I am choosing to live. Operate on me as if I am alive, not dead."

Jerry lived thanks to the skill of his doctors, but also because of his amazing attitude. I learned from him that every day we have the choice to live fully. So remember, change your attitude to change your life.

Think of how the above story applies to your sport. Athletes make a lot of mistakes through the course of a season. After each mistake, we have a choice of how to respond. As Jerry said, you can choose to complain or you can look at the positive side of things. You have two choices.

## What Did You Learn Today?

I've learned- that you cannot make someone love you. All
you can do is be someone who can be loved. The
rest is up to them.

I've learned- that no matter how much I care, some people
just don't care back.

I've learned- that it takes years to build up trust, and only
seconds to destroy it.

I've learned- that it's not what you have in your life but
who you have in your life that counts.

I've learned- that you can get by on charm for about fifteen
minutes. After that, you'd better know something.

I've learned- that you shouldn't compare yourself to the
best others can do.

I've learned- that you can do something in an instant that
will give you heartache for life.

I've learned- that it's taking me a long time to become the
person I want to be.

I've learned- that you can keep going long after you can' t.

I've learned- that we are responsible for what we do, no
matter how we feel.

I've learned- that either you control your attitude or it con-
trols you.

I've learned- that heroes are the people who do what has to be done when it needs to be done, regardless of the consequences.

I've learned- that money is a lousy way of keeping score.

I've learned- that sometimes the people you expect to kick you when you're down will be the ones to help you get back up.

I've learned- that sometimes when I'm angry I have the right to be angry, but that doesn't give me the right to be cruel.

I've learned- that you should never tell a child their dreams are unlikely or outlandish. Few things are more humiliating, and what a tragedy it would be if they believed it.

I've learned- that no matter how good a friend is, they're going to hurt you every once in a while and you must forgive them for that.

I've learned- that it isn't always enough to be forgiven by others. Sometimes you have to learn to forgive yourself.

I've learned- that no matter how bad your heart is broken the world doesn't stop for your grief.

I've learned- that our background and circumstances may have influenced who we are, but we are responsible for who we become.

I've learned- that just because two people argue, it doesn't mean they don't love each other. And just because they don't argue, it doesn't mean they do.

I've learned- that we don't have to change friends if we understand that friends change.

I've learned- that two people can look at the exact same thing and see something totally different.

I've learned- that even when you think you have no more to give, when a friend cries out to you, you will find the strength to help.

I've learned- that credentials on the wall do not make you a decent human being.

I've learned- that it's hard to determine where to draw the line between being nice and not hurting people's feelings and standing up for what you believe.

I've learned- that maturity has more to do with what types of experiences you've had and what you've learned from them and less to do with how many birthdays you've celebrated.

As you learn more of life's lessons, right them here and share them with others.

## Do It Anyway...

People are often unreasonable, illogical, and self-centered;

Forgive them anyway.

If you are kind, people may accuse you of selfish, ulterior motives;

Be kind anyway.

If you give generously, people will probably try to take advantage of you.

Give generously anyway.

If you are successful, you will win some false friends and some true enemies;

Succeed anyway.

If you are honest and frank, people may scoff at you;

Be honest and frank anyway.

What you spend years building, someone could destroy overnight;

Build anyway.

If you find serenity and happiness, they may be jealous;

Be happy anyway.

The good you do today, people will often forget tomorrow;

> Do good anyway.

Give the world the best you have, and it may never be enough;

> Give the world the best you have anyway.

You see, in the final analysis, it is between you and God;

It never was between you and them anyway.

## 5 Short Stories: Important Things Life Teaches You

### 1~ Most Important Question

During my second month of nursing school, our professor gave us a pop quiz. I was a conscientious student and had breezed through the questions, until I read the last one: "What is the first name of the woman who cleans the school?" Surely this was some kind of joke. I had seen the cleaning woman several times. She was tall, dark-haired and in her 50s, but how would I know her name? I handed in my paper, leaving the last question blank. Before class ended, one student asked if the last question would count toward our quiz grade. "Absolutely," said the professor. "In your careers you will meet many people. All are significant. They deserve your attention and care, even if all you do is smile and say 'Hello'. "I've never forgotten that lesson. I also learned her name was Dorothy.

### 2 ~ Pickup in the Rain

One night, at 11:30 PM, an older African American woman was standing on the side of an Alabama highway trying to endure a lashing rainstorm. Her car had broken down and she desperately needed a ride. Soaking wet, she decided to flag down the next car. A young white man stopped to help her - generally unheard of in those conflict-filled 1960s. The man took her to safety, helped her get assistance and put her into a taxicab. She seemed to be in a big hurry! She wrote down his address, thanked him and drove away. Seven days went by and a knock came on the man's door. To his surprise, a giant console color TV was delivered to his home. A special note was attached. It read: "Thank you so much for assisting me on the highway the other night. The rain drenched not only my clothes but also my spirits. Then you came along. Because of you, I was able to make it to my dying husband's bedside just before he passed away. God bless you for helping me and unselfishly serving others." Sincerely, Mrs. Nat King Cole

## 3 ~ Always Remember Those Who Serve

In the days when an ice cream sundae cost much less, a 10 year old boy entered a hotel coffee shop and sat at a table. A waitress put a glass of water in front of him. "How much is an ice cream sundae?" "Fifty cents," replied the waitress. The little boy pulled his hand out of his pocket and studied a number of coins in it. "How much is a dish of plain ice cream?" he inquired. Some people were now waiting for a table and the waitress was a bit impatient. "Thirty-five cents," she said brusquely. The little boy again counted the coins. "I'll have the plain ice cream," he said. The waitress brought the ice cream, put the bill on the table and walked away. The boy finished the ice cream, paid the cashier and departed. When the waitress came back, she began wiping down the table and then swallowed hard at what she saw. There, placed neatly beside the empty dish, were two nickels and five pennies - her tip.

## 4 ~ The Obstacle in Our Path

In ancient times, a king had a boulder placed on a roadway. Then he hid himself and watched to see if anyone would remove the huge rock. Some of the king's wealthiest merchants and courtiers came by and simply walked around it. Many loudly blamed the king for not keeping the roads clear, but none did anything about getting the big stone out of the way. Then a peasant came along carrying a load of vegetables. On approaching the boulder, the peasant laid down his burden and tried to move the stone to the side of the road. After much pushing and straining, he finally succeeded. As the peasant picked up his load of vegetables, he noticed a purse lying in the road where the boulder had been. The purse contained many gold coins and a note from the king indicating that the gold was for the person who removed the boulder from the roadway. The peasant learned what many others never understand.

Every obstacle presents an opportunity to improve one's condition.

## 5 ~ Giving Blood

Many years ago, when I worked as a volunteer at Stanford Hospital, I got to know a little girl named Liz who was suffering from a rare and serious disease. Her only chance of recovery appeared to be a blood transfusion from her 5-year old brother, who had miraculously survived the same disease and had developed the antibodies, needed to combat the illness. The doctor explained the situation to her little brother, and asked the boy if he would be willing to give his blood to his sister. I saw him hesitate for only a moment before taking a deep breath and saying, "Yes, I'll do it if it will save Liz." As the transfusion progressed, he lay in bed next to his sister. He looked up at the doctor and asked with a trembling voice, "Will I start to die right away?" Being young, the boy had misunderstood the doctor; he thought he was going to have to give his sister all of his blood.

## ALL Your Strength

One day a small boy was trying to lift a heavy stone, but he couldn't budge it. His father, passing by, stopped to watch his efforts. Finally, he said to his son: "Are you using all your strength?"

"Yes, I am," the boy cried, exasperated.

"No," the father said calmly, "you're not. You haven't asked me to help you."

Mental effort is just as important as physical effort.

## I Want to Know

**I Want to Know,** by Oriah Mountain Dreamer (A Native American Elder)

It doesn't interest me what you do for a living. I want to know what you ache for, and if you dare dream of meeting your heart's longing.

It doesn't interest me how old you are. I want to know if you will risk looking the fool for love, for your dreams, for the adventure of being alive.

It doesn't interest me what planets are squaring your moon. I want to know if you have touched the center of your sorrow, if you have been opened up by life's betrayals or have become shriveled and closed from fear of further pain.

I want to know if you can sit with pain, mine or your own, if you can dance with wildness and let ecstasy fill you to the tips of your fingers and toes without cautioning us to be careful, be realistic, or to remember the limitations of being human.

It doesn't interest me if the story you are telling me is true. I want to know if you can betray another to be true to yourself; if you can bear the accusation of betrayal and not betray your own soul. I want to know if you can be faithful and therefore be trustworthy. I want to know if you can see beauty even when it's not a pretty day.

I want to know if you can live with failure, yours and mine, and stand on the edge of a lake and shout to the silver light of a full moon, "Yes!"

It doesn't interest me to know where you live or how much money you have. I want to know if you can get up after a night of grief and despair, weary and bruised to the bone, and do what needs to be done for the children.

It doesn't matter who you are, or how you came to be here. I want to know if you will stand in the center of the fire with me and not shrink back.

It doesn't interest me where or what or with whom you have studied. I want to know what sustains you from the inside when all else falls away. I want to know if you can be alone with yourself, and if you truly like the company you keep in the empty moments.

## The Value of Time

A man came home from work late again, tired and irritated, to find his five-year-old son waiting for him at the door.

"Daddy, may I ask you a question?" "Yeah, sure. What is it?" replied the man. "Daddy, how much money do you make an hour?"

"That's none of your business! What makes you ask such a thing?" the man said angrily. "I just want to know. Please tell me, how much do you make an hour?" pleaded the little boy.

"If you must know, I make $20 an hour." "Oh," the little boy replied, head bowed. Looking up, he said: "Daddy, may I borrow $10 please?"

The father was furious. "If the only reason you wanted to know how much money I make is just so you can borrow some to buy a silly toy or some other nonsense, then you march yourself straight to your room and go to bed. Think about why you're being so selfish. I work long, hard hours everyday and don't have time for such childish games."

The little boy quietly went to his room and shut the door. The man sat down and started to get even madder about the little boy's questioning. How dare he ask such questions only to get some money! After an hour or so, the man had calmed down, and started to think he may have been a little hard on his son. Maybe there was something he really needed to buy with that $10, and he really didn't ask for money very often.

The man went to the door of the little boy's room and opened the door. "Are you asleep son?" he asked. "No, daddy, I'm awake," replied the boy. "I've been thinking, maybe I was too hard on you earlier," said the man. "It's been a long day and I took my anger out on you.  Here's that $10 you asked for."

The little boy sat straight up, beaming.  "Oh, thank you, daddy!" he yelled. Then, reaching under his pillow, he pulled out some more crumpled up bills. The man, seeing that the boy already had money, started to get angry again. The little boy slowly counted out his money, then looked up at the man.  "Why did you want more money if you already had some?" the father grumbled. Because I didn't have enough, but now I do," the little boy replied. "Daddy, I have $20 now. Can I buy an hour of your time?"

Time is the most valuable thing we have. Everyone has the same amount of it, just some value it more than others. Spend your time wisely.

## A Commencement Speech

I have no specialized field of interest or expertise, which puts me at a disadvantage talking to you today. I'm a novelist. My work is human nature. Real life is all I know. Don't ever confuse the two, your life and your work. The second is only part of the first. Don't ever forget what a friend once wrote Senator Paul Tsongas when the senator decided not to run for re-election because he had been diagnosed with cancer: "No man ever said on his deathbed I wish I had spent more time at the office."

Don't ever forget the words my father sent me on a postcard last year: "If you win the rat race, you're still a rat." Or what John Lennon wrote before he was gunned down in the driveway of the Dakota: "Life is what happens while you are busy making other plans." You will walk out of here this afternoon with only one thing that no one else has. There will be hundreds of people out there with your same degree; there will be thousands of people doing what you want to do for a living. But you will be the only person alive who has sole custody of your life. Your particular life. Your entire life. Not just your life at a desk, or your life on a bus, or in a car, or at the computer. Not just the life of your mind, but the life of your heart. Not just your bank account but your soul. People don't talk about the soul very much anymore. It's so much easier to write a resume than to craft a spirit. But a resume is a cold comfort on a winter night, or when you're sad, or broke, or lonely, or when you've gotten back the test results and they're not so good.

Here is my resume: I am a good mother to three children. I have tried never to let my profession stand in the way of being a good parent. I no longer consider myself the center of the universe. I show up. I listen. I try to laugh. I am a good friend to my husband. I have tried to make marriage vows

99

mean what they say. I am a good friend to my friends, and they to me. Without them, there would be nothing to say to you today, because I would be a cardboard cutout. But I call them on the phone, and I meet them for lunch. I would be rotten, or at best mediocre at my job, if those other things were not true. You cannot be really first rate at your work if your work is all you are. So here's what I wanted to tell you today: Get a life...a real life, not manic pursuit of the next promotion, the bigger paycheck, the larger house. Do you think you'd care so very much about those things if you blew an aneurysm one afternoon, or found a lump in your breast?

Get a life in which you notice the smell of salt water pushing itself on breeze over Seaside Heights, a life in which you stop and watch how a red-tailed hawk circles over the water or the way a baby scowls with concentration when she tries to pick up a Cheerio with her thumb and first finger. Get a life in which you are not alone. Find people you love, and who love you. And remember that love is not leisure, it is work. Pick up the phone. Send an e-mail. Write a letter. Get a life in which you are generous. And realize that life is the best thing ever, and that you have no business taking it for granted. Care so deeply about its goodness that you want to spread it around. Take money you would have spent on beers and give it to charity. Work in a soup kitchen. Be a big brother or sister. All of you want to do well. But if you do not do good too, then doing well will never be enough. It is so easy to waste our lives, our days, our hours, our minutes. It is so easy to take for granted the color of our kids' eyes, the way the melody in a symphony rises and falls and disappears and rises again. It is so easy to exist instead of to live.

I learned to live many years ago. Something really, really bad happened to me, something that changed my life in ways that, if I had my druthers, it would never have been changed at all. And what I learned from it is what, today, seems to be the hardest lesson of all. I learned to love the journey, not the destination. I learned that it is not a dress rehearsal, and that today is the only guarantee you get. I learned to look at all the good in the world and try to give some of it back because I believed in it completely and utterly. And I tried to do that, in part, by telling others what I had learned. By telling them this: Consider the lilies of the field. Look at the fuzz on a baby's ear. Read in the backyard with the sun on your face.

Learn to be happy. And think of life as a terminal illness, because if you do, you will live it with joy and passion, as it ought to be lived.

## The Paradox of Our Time: By George Carlin

The paradox of our time in history is that we have taller buildings but shorter tempers; wider freeways, but narrower viewpoints. We spend more, but have less; we buy more but enjoy less. We have bigger houses and smaller families, more conveniences, but less time; we have more degrees, but less sense; more knowledge, but less judgment; more experts, yet more problems, more medicine, but less wellness. We drink too much, smoke too much, spend too recklessly, laugh too little, drive too fast, get too angry, stay up too late, get up too tired, read too little, watch TV too much, and pray too seldom. We have multiplied our possessions, but reduced our values.

We talk too much, love too seldom, and hate too often. We've learned how to make a living, but not a life, we've added years to life not life to years. We've been all the way to the moon and back, but have trouble crossing the street to meet a new neighbor. We conquered outer space but not inner space. We've done larger things, but not better things. We've cleaned up the air, but polluted the soul. We've conquered the atom, but not our prejudice. We write more, but learn less. We plan more, but accomplish less. We've learned to rush, but not to wait. We build more computers to hold more information to produce more copies than ever, but we communicate less and less.

These are the times of fast foods and slow digestion; big men and small character; steep profits and shallow relationships. These are the days of two incomes but more divorce, fancier houses but broken homes. These are days of quick trips, disposable diapers, throw-away morality, one-night stands, overweight bodies, and pills that do everything from cheer to quiet, to kill. It is a time when there is much in the show window and nothing in the stockroom! A time when technology can bring this letter to you, and a time when you can choose either to share this insight, or to just hit delete.

Remember, spend some time with your loved ones, because they are not going to be around forever. Remember, say a kind word to someone who looks up to you in awe, because that little person soon will grow up and leave your side. Remember, to give a warm hug to the one next to you, because that is the only treasure you can give with your heart and it doesn't cost a cent. Remember, to say "I Love you" to your partner and your loved ones, but most of all mean it. A kiss and an embrace will mend hurt when it comes from deep inside of you. Remember to hold hands and cherish the moment for someday that person will not be there again. Give time to Love, give time to speak, give time to share the precious thoughts in your mind.

Work like you don't need the money. Love like you've never been hurt. And Dance, yes dance like no one is watching.

## Quotes from John Wooden

John Wooden is widely accepted as one of the greatest coaches of all time. He coached the UCLA men's basketball team to a record number of national championships. He stressed hard work and teamwork. His practices were always challenging and even though his players were not the best athletes, most of them went on to play at the professional level. Coach Wooden has often said that his greatest accomplishment was his players – "they developed into phenomenal people."

1. Fear no opponent. Respect every opponent.

2. Remember, it's the perfection of the smallest details that makes big things happen.

3. Keep in mind that hustle makes up for many a mistake.

4. Be more interested in your character than your reputation.

5. Be quick, but don't hurry.

6. Understand that the harder you work, the more luck you will have.

7. Know that valid self-analysis is crucial for improvement.

8. Remember that there is no substitute for hard work and careful planning. Failing to prepare is preparing to fail.

Roadmap to the Zone customers:  single-step.com

# Start setting your goals now!

single-step

http://www.single-step.com/roadmap/offer.html

CPN4522582755

Printed in the United States
20978LVS00003B/454-591